Who Was Johnny Appleseed?

Who Was
Johnny
Appleseed?

By Joan Holub
Illustrated by Anna DiVito

Grosset & Dunlap

For Liz and Lamar Cole—J.H.
For Pearl—A.D.

GROSSET & DUNLAP
Published by the Penguin Group
Penguin Group (USA) Inc., 375 Hudson Street, New York, New York 10014, U.S.A.
Penguin Group (Canada), 10 Alcorn Avenue, Toronto, Ontario, Canada M4V 3B2
(a division of Pearson Penguin Canada Inc.)
Penguin Books Ltd, 80 Strand, London WC2R 0RL, England
Penguin Ireland, 25 St Stephen's Green, Dublin 2, Ireland (a division of Penguin Books Ltd)
Penguin Group (Australia), 250 Camberwell Road, Camberwell, Victoria 3124, Australia
(a division of Pearson Australia Group Pty Ltd)
Penguin Books India Pvt Ltd, 11 Community Centre, Panchsheel Park, New Delhi - 110 017, India
Penguin Group (NZ), Cnr Airborne and Rosedale Roads, Albany, Auckland 1310, New Zealand
(a division of Pearson New Zealand Ltd)
Penguin Books (South Africa) (Pty) Ltd, 24 Sturdee Avenue, Rosebank, Johannesburg 2196, South Africa

Penguin Books Ltd, Registered Offices: 80 Strand, London WC2R 0RL, England

Library of Congress Cataloging-in-Publication Data

Holub, Joan.
  Who was Johnny Appleseed? / by Joan Holub ; illustrated by Anna DiVito.
    p. cm. — (Who was—?)
Includes bibliographical references.
  ISBN 978-0-448-43968-6
  1. Appleseed, Johnny, 1774-1845. 2. Apple growers—United States—Biography. 3. Frontier and
pioneer life—Middle West. I. DiVito, Anna, ill. II. Title. III. Series.
  SB63.C46H66 2005
  634'.11'092—dc22

                    2005003383

30 29 28 27 26 25 24 23 22

Contents

Who Was
Johnny Appleseed?

Johnny Appleseed's real name was John Chapman. He earned his nickname by planting thousands of apple seeds in America's Midwest. For this, he became a legend during his own lifetime.

Johnny Appleseed was best known as an apple lover, but he was many other things as well.

He was a peacemaker who tried to calm the trouble between settlers and Native Americans.

He was a religious person who preached to pioneers.

He was a friend to animals and helped forest creatures whenever he could.

He was an eccentric person. That means he did things differently from most other people.

He lived alone in the wilderness. He never settled in one place. And he dressed oddly—really oddly. Settlers always remembered meeting him because he stood out.

He was a storyteller. When Johnny visited pioneer cabins to sell apple seedlings, he talked about his adventures on the frontier. The settlers told his stories to other settlers. Over time, some of his stories were exaggerated or changed. By now, it's sometimes hard to separate the tales from the truth.

What is the real story behind the legend of Johnny Appleseed?

Chapter 1
Young Johnny

It was September 26, 1774, in Leominster, Massachusetts. Colonists were just beginning to pick newly ripened apples from their trees. Nathaniel and Elizabeth Chapman were celebrating. Their

first son was born that day. They named him John, but someday he would be better known as Johnny Appleseed.

Johnny also had a sister named Elizabeth. She was four years old. The family was poor and lived in a small house they rented from relatives. Though Johnny's father did farming and carpentry work, he wasn't very successful.

THE BOSTON TEA PARTY

TODAY, AMERICANS DRINK MORE COFFEE THAN
TEA. BUT IN JOHNNY APPLESEED'S TIME, IT WAS THE
OTHER WAY AROUND. TEA WAS MORE POPULAR. SO
THE COLONISTS GOT REALLY MAD WHEN THE ENGLISH
GOVERNMENT PUT A TAX ON IT.

BEGINNING IN 1765, ENGLAND SAID COLONISTS HAD
TO PAY TAXES ON IMPORTED GLASS, LEAD, PAINT,
PAPER, AND TEA. COLONISTS DIDN'T WANT TO BE
TAXED IF THEY WEREN'T ALLOWED ANY SAY IN
MAKING LAWS. THEY DID EVERYTHING THEY
COULD TO AVOID PAYING THE TAXES.

ON DECEMBER 16, 1773, A GROUP
OF COLONISTS DECIDED TO
PROTEST THE

TEA TAX IN A BIG WAY. DISGUISED AS MEMBERS OF THE MOHAWK TRIBE, THEY SNEAKED ONTO SHIPS DOCKED IN BOSTON HARBOR. THE SHIPS WERE LOADED WITH 342 BOXES OF TEA. MANY COLONISTS LIKED TEA SO MUCH THAT THEY HAD A HARD TIME DOING WITHOUT IT. TO STOP ANYONE FROM BUYING THE TEA, THESE MEN TOSSED IT OVERBOARD.

THIS PROTEST BECAME KNOWN AS THE BOSTON TEA PARTY. IT HAPPENED JUST FIFTY MILES FROM LEOMINSTER, WHERE JOHNNY WAS BORN NINE MONTHS LATER.

Shortly before Johnny was born, his father had taken on yet a third job. At that time, many colonists wanted to go to war against England. They hoped to break away and form a new country. Like many of these patriots, Johnny's father became a minuteman. Minutemen promised to defend the thirteen colonies from English troops at a minute's notice.

When Johnny was less than a year old, his father was called to duty. He helped fight the English at the battle of Bunker Hill.

By the spring of 1776, his father was marching with George Washington's army. That

July, the Declaration of Independence was signed. The colonies were fighting for independence from England in the Revolutionary War.

That same year, before Johnny's second birthday, something terrible happened. His mother and newborn brother died. Johnny was probably too young to understand what was going on, but he no doubt missed his mother. Since their father was still in the army, Johnny and his sister went to live with their grandparents.

At the age of five, Johnny got a new stepmother. His father married a woman named Lucy Cooley and left the army. The family of four moved to the nearby town of Longmeadow.

Ten more children were born into the Chapman family over the following years. Imagine such a big family living in one small farmhouse!

To get some peace and quiet, Johnny spent much of his time outside. The Connecticut River flowed near his house and a forest grew nearby.

THE CHAPMAN FAMILY

NATHANIEL

ELIZABETH

JOHNNY

NATHANIEL

PATTY

PERSIS

MARY

LUCY

ABNER

PIERLY

LUCY

JONATHAN

DAVIS

SALLY

Johnny felt more at home outdoors than he did in the overcrowded farmhouse. In the woods, he could be as free as the Native Americans and woodsmen that roamed the frontier.

There was a school in Longmeadow, which Johnny attended for a few years. There he learned to write in a handwriting style called "round

hand." He learned to love books, as he would for the rest of his life.

Boys could get jobs to earn money at age fourteen. Johnny probably learned how to grow apples by working in an apple orchard when he was a teenager. His interest in apples began to blossom.

A PIONEER SCHOOL

SOME CHILDREN IN THE FRONTIER DIDN'T GO TO SCHOOL AND NEVER LEARNED TO READ OR WRITE. OTHERS WERE TAUGHT AT HOME BY THEIR PARENTS. IF AN AREA HAD A SCHOOL, THE SCHOOLHOUSE WAS USUALLY ONLY ONE ROOM IN WHICH STUDENTS OF ALL AGES WERE TAUGHT READING, WRITING, AND MATH.

STUDENTS USUALLY HAD TO BRING THEIR OWN BOOKS, CALLED PRIMERS, READERS, OR SPELLERS. NOAH WEBSTER'S *AMERICAN SPELLING BOOK*, PUBLISHED IN 1783, CONTAINED LISTS OF VOCABULARY WORDS AND STORIES THAT TAUGHT GOOD BEHAVIOR.

IF THERE WERE NOT ENOUGH PRIMERS, STUDENTS LEARNED FROM A HORNBOOK. A HORNBOOK WAS A WOODEN PADDLE THAT HELD A PIECE OF PAPER ON EACH SIDE. A SEE-THROUGH SHEET OF ANIMAL HORN COVERED THE PAPERS, WHICH WERE PRINTED WITH LESSONS. THIS PROTECTED THEM SO THEY COULD BE STUDIED OVER AND OVER.

THE TEACHER MADE PENS FOR STUDENTS OUT OF GOOSE FEATHERS. ONE END OF THE FEATHER WAS SHARPENED WITH A KNIFE AND DIPPED IN INK FOR WRITING. IT COULD TAKE TWO HOURS TO MAKE ENOUGH PENS FOR THE WHOLE CLASS. PIONEERS MADE THEIR OWN INK BY MIXING INK POWDER, VINEGAR, AND WATER.

Chapter 2
Johnny's Big Idea

The main road through Longmeadow was busy. People traveling to and from Connecticut and New York brought news.

In 1783 Johnny learned that the Revolutionary War was officially over. The colonies had finally gotten what they wanted—independence. Now all land from the colonies to the Mississippi River belonged to the colonists, except for Florida, which Spain owned.

When Johnny was about twelve, the new United States organized

the Northwest Territory so that government land
could be sold to settlers in smaller pieces.

The territory was bordered by the Mississippi River, the Ohio River, and the Great Lakes. (It later became the states of Illinois, Indiana, Michigan, Ohio, Wisconsin, and part of Minnesota.)

A group of land developers formed the Ohio Company and bought 1.5 million acres of Ohio land. In 1788 they sent forty-eight pioneers to begin the town of Marietta, Ohio. This became the first permanent pioneer settlement in the Northwest Territory.

BRITISH TERRITORY

NORTHWEST TERRITORY

MISSISSIPPI RIVER

SPANISH LOUISIANA

NY

PA

VA

KY

TN

NORTHWEST TERRITORY

Over the next few years, Johnny watched settlers pass through town. They were moving west in search of a better life.

Farmland, lumber, and food weren't as plentiful in the area as they had once been. In Johnny Appleseed's time, farmers didn't fertilize land. When  their soil lost its richness after many seasons of growing crops, they looked for fresh farmland. Back then, people didn't conserve forestland or protect animal populations either. As nearby forests were logged and animals hunted, people had to go farther from home in search of lumber and food.

They left on wagons, horseback, and foot to establish farms. At that time, when pioneers said they were "going west," they were heading for what is now Ohio or Indiana. Today, these states are called the "Midwest."

Johnny knew settlers would want fruit when they got to the west. Apples had many uses, and lots of people grew them. But settlers wouldn't have room in their wagons for bags of apple seeds or seedlings. That gave him an idea.

Cider mills located in many towns mashed the juice out of leftover apples. A drink called

apple cider was made from the juice. The cores of the apples were thrown away. Johnny thought this was a waste.

After all, apple cores had apple seeds. And he could have the cider mills' seeds for free! Maybe he could take them westward and start an apple-tree-growing business.

INSIDE A COVERED WAGON

IF YOU COULD TAKE ONLY A FEW OF YOUR THINGS ON A TRIP, WHAT WOULD YOU TAKE? WHAT WOULD YOU LEAVE BEHIND? PIONEERS MOVING WEST HAD TO MAKE HARD CHOICES.

THEY SOLD THEIR HOMES BEFORE MOVING WEST. IF THEY HAD CHICKENS, PIGS, OR OTHER LIVESTOCK, THEY USUALLY SOLD THOSE, TOO. CHILDREN OFTEN HAD TO LEAVE BELOVED PETS OR TOYS BEHIND.

THE FLOOR OF A COVERED WAGON WAS ABOUT FOUR FEET WIDE AND SIX TO TEN FEET LONG. THAT'S ABOUT THE SIZE OF A DOUBLE BED! WAGONS WERE USED FOR SLEEPING, RIDING, AND STORAGE.

APPLES IN PIONEER TIMES

THE THREE MAIN FOODS PIONEERS ATE WERE MEAT, CORN, AND APPLES. THEY HARVESTED APPLES EVERY FALL AND ATE MANY OF THEM RIGHT AWAY. SOME, THEY BAKED INTO PIES OR BOILED TO MAKE APPLE BUTTER.

OTHERS, THEY CRUSHED TO MAKE APPLE CIDER. BEFORE THEY HAD RUNNING WATER, COLONISTS DRANK A LOT OF THAT. WITHIN A FEW MONTHS AFTER THE HARVEST, LEFTOVER APPLES STARTED TO ROT. THIS WAS A PROBLEM. PIONEERS DIDN'T WANT TO GO WITHOUT FRUIT ALL WINTER.

FRESHLY CUT APPLES TURN BROWN QUICKLY. THAT'S BECAUSE CHEMICALS IN AN APPLE REACT WITH OXYGEN IN THE AIR. THIS CHEMICAL REACTION IS CALLED "OXIDATION." OXIDATION IS ALSO WHAT CAUSES IRON OBJECTS TO RUST.

ONCE ITS JUICE IS REMOVED, AN APPLE WON'T ROT. ONE WAY PIONEERS DRIED APPLE SLICES WAS BY PLACING THEM IN A SMALL ROOM CALLED A "DRYHOUSE." A WOOD FIRE DRIED THE APPLES, WHICH LAY ON SHELVES MADE OF SCREENS.

ANOTHER WAY WAS BY SETTING APPLE SLICES ON OUTDOOR TABLES TO DRY IN THE SUN. WASPS AND BEES HELPED SUCK THE JUICE OUT OF THEM!

PIONEERS TIED THEIR DRIED APPLES TOGETHER ON STRINGS AND HUNG THEM FROM THE KITCHEN CEILING UNTIL NEEDED FOR COOKING.

Chapter 3
Planting the First Seeds

When he was twenty-three years old, Johnny made his move. No one knows why he finally decided to head west. Maybe he'd heard that the Holland Land Company was selling land in Pennsylvania. Maybe he'd heard promises that treaties with the Native Americans had made travel safer.

Whatever his reason, he began hiking west toward Pennsylvania in 1797. His supplies included a gun, an ax, and a bag of food. He walked barefoot and probably

stuck to smaller trails, which he liked better than main roads.

Several new towns were forming in the Pennsylvania wilderness. River transportation was easier than overland transportation in those days. So most early settlements began along rivers. Johnny headed for the town of Warren on the Allegheny River.

The weather was good when he started out that November. But as he reached northwestern Pennsylvania's Allegheny Mountains, it began to snow. He tore cloth strips from his coat, wrapped them around his feet, and walked on.

Soon the snow was three feet deep. It was dangerously cold and getting too hard to walk. Johnny pulled branches from nearby beech trees and wove them together. He couldn't stop for long or he'd

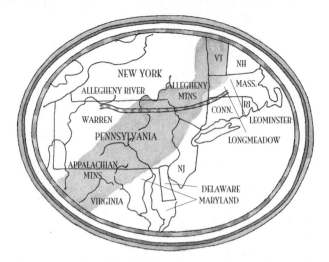

freeze to death. Quickly, he made a pair of crude snowshoes. He strapped them to his feet and walked out of the snowstorm.

When Johnny reached Warren, he discovered it wasn't much of a town. It turned out to be just one log cabin with a land salesman living inside. Still, he was probably glad to find shelter for a while.

Johnny had already collected apple seeds from cider mills he passed in Pennsylvania. That winter, he explored the area around Warren in search of a good place to grow apple trees. He didn't aimlessly scatter his apple seeds everywhere, as some people think. He planned to plant small fruit farms called orchards.

By the spring, he had chosen a good spot. He planted his first orchard along the Brokenstraw River, which branched off from the Allegheny River just west of Warren.

There were rules for claiming land in Pennsylvania. You had to pay for it, for one thing. But that wasn't all. You also had to build a cabin and raise a crop on it. Johnny tried to establish land claims but found that doing so was hard. Land boundaries were unclear and laws were confusing.

So like many other frontier settlers, Johnny became a squatter. That meant he didn't buy or lease land. He planted on land owned by others or on unclaimed government land. Some landowners lived far away and never knew he was using their land. He made deals with other landowners to trade part of his crop for use of their land.

Unfortunately, the market for apples wasn't very good in Warren. Within a year, he planted another orchard. It was located fifty miles southwest on the Allegheny River, near the town of Franklin. Many settlers passed through Franklin on their way west. It was a better market for his apples, and he worked there several years.

Except for visits from his half brother Nathaniel, Johnny's life was hard and lonely at this time. He slept in hollow trees or under blankets of leaves. One winter, he only had nuts to eat.

DANIEL BOONE
(1734–1820)

DANIEL BOONE WAS BORN IN 1734, FORTY YEARS BEFORE JOHNNY APPLESEED. LIKE JOHNNY, HE SPENT MUCH OF HIS LIFE ROAMING THE WOODS OF THE FRONTIER. UNLIKE JOHNNY, DANIEL MADE HIS LIVING HUNTING AND TRAPPING BEAR, DEER, BEAVER, AND OTTERS.

IN 1769 DANIEL FOUND A SECRET PASSAGE THROUGH KENTUCKY'S CUMBERLAND MOUNTAINS. HE HELPED BUILD THE WILDERNESS ROAD, WHICH LED THROUGH A MOUNTAIN GAP. THIS WAS A BIG HELP TO PIONEERS BECAUSE THE GAP WAS WIDE ENOUGH FOR THEIR WAGONS TO PASS THROUGH. THE CUMBERLAND GAP BECAME ONE OF THE GATEWAYS TO THE WEST.

Chapter 4
Johnny Takes Care of His Orchards

Johnny's orchards kept him busy year-round.

Every fall, Pennsylvania farmers took their newly picked apples to the cider mills. So that's when seeds were plentiful. Johnny usually collected a couple of bushels of them from the mills.

During the winter, Johnny fixed his orchard fences. These kept deer and other animals from nibbling on his trees.

Each spring and summer, he tended his orchards. He also chose sites for new orchards. He cleared the land, chopping shrubs and pulling weeds. He tilled the soil, then carefully planted apple seeds.

Squirrels and mice always ate some of the seeds before they could sprout. But he didn't mind. He left the seeds to grow and came back later to check on them.

All year long, Johnny was also a traveling salesman. He went door-to-door, visiting settlers' cabins. He sold apple seeds and seedlings.

HOW APPLES GROW

EVERY SPRING, BUDS FORM ON THE BRANCHES OF AN APPLE TREE. THE BUDS BLOOM INTO FLOWERS CALLED BLOSSOMS, WHICH OFTEN GROW IN GROUPS OF FIVE. MOST APPLE BLOSSOMS ARE PINK AT FIRST BUT SOON TURN WHITE. EACH BLOSSOM HAS FIVE PETALS, WHICH FALL OFF AFTER ONLY A FEW DAYS. A GREEN BALL, WHICH IS A BABY APPLE, GROWS IN PLACE OF EACH BLOSSOM. BY FALL, THESE APPLES ARE BIG ENOUGH TO PICK AND EAT. APPLES ARE PICKED BY HAND BECAUSE HARVESTING MACHINES WOULD BRUISE THEM. THEY ARE WASHED AND PACKED IN CRATES. REFRIGERATED TRUCKS OR TRAINS DELIVER THEM TO STORES.

YOU CAN GROW A TREE FROM THE SEED OF AN APPLE YOU EAT. THE TREE WILL TAKE FIVE OR MORE YEARS TO PRODUCE ITS FIRST FRUIT. BUT THE TREE'S APPLES WILL NOT TASTE AS GOOD AS THE APPLE YOU ATE. APPLE TREES SHOULD BE GROWN IN GROUPS. BEES CROSS-POLLINATE SWEET SMELLING APPLE FLOWERS, RESULTING IN BETTER-TASTING APPLES. APPLE GROWERS USUALLY PUT BEEHIVES IN THEIR ORCHARDS EACH SPRING.

An apple seedling is a small plant that sprouts from an apple seed. It will grow into an apple tree. He sold them for six and one-half cents each.

Settlers had a good reason for wanting to buy Johnny's apple seedlings. If they planted apple seeds themselves, they would have to wait two years for four-foot-tall seedlings. With Johnny's help, settlers got a head start on growing apples.

When settlers planted an orchard from seeds, they never knew exactly what kind of apples they'd get from the trees. That's because of pollination. When an apple tree is flowering, bees spread pollen among different blossoms, resulting in trees with new types of apples.

Many farmers grafted trees together to improve apple crops. "Grafting" means joining two plants together. First, they cut a branch from a tree that had apples they liked. Then they tied that branch to a seedling grown from a different type of apple. The two parts eventually grew into a tree with a new kind of apple. Almost all apple trees are grafted today.

Johnny knew grafting was a better way to grow apples. But he thought it was wrong. He believed that only God should decide how apples develop. So he always grew his trees from seeds instead of grafting. His apples were wild apples, which weren't as tasty as most apples in stores today.

PARTS OF AN APPLE BLOSSOM

THE PISTIL IS IN THE MIDDLE OF AN APPLE
BLOSSOM. IT IS THE FEMALE PART, WHICH INCLUDES
THE STIGMAS, STYLES, AND OVULES. THE OVULES
WILL BECOME SEEDS ONCE THEY ARE FERTILIZED WITH
POLLEN FROM ANOTHER FLOWER.

THE STAMENS ARE THE MALE PART OF THE FLOWER
WHERE POLLEN IS FOUND. MOST POLLEN IS YELLOW.

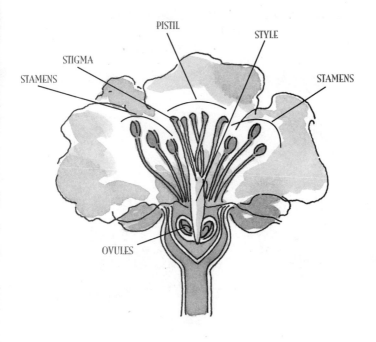

A BEE POLLINATES AN APPLE BLOSSOM

1. A HONEYBEE LANDS ON THE PETALS OF AN APPLE BLOSSOM. IT COLLECTS POWDER, CALLED POLLEN, IN TINY SACS ON ITS BACK LEGS.

2. THE BEE FLIES TO ANOTHER BLOSSOM WHERE IT GATHERS MORE POLLEN. SOME OF THE POLLEN FROM THE FIRST BLOSSOM STICKS TO THE STIGMAS OF THE SECOND BLOSSOM. THIS ALLOWS THE NEW BLOSSOM TO MAKE SEEDS. BLOSSOMS CANNOT POLLINATE THEMSELVES. THEY NEED HONEYBEES TO HELP SPREAD THE POLLEN FROM BLOSSOM TO BLOSSOM.

Chapter 5
The Apple Business Grows

In 1800, the census counted 5.3 million people in the United States. Pennsylvania was getting too crowded to suit Johnny.

When he was twenty-six, he led a horse across the Pennsylvania border into Ohio. It was

carrying a load of apple seeds. He planted his first Ohio orchard near the town of Carrollton. He would plant many more orchards in north and central Ohio.

At this time, most of Ohio was still a forested wilderness full of bears and other wild animals. Not many people lived there, and the ones who did were rough and wild. Johnny had grown up in the colonies, so he stood out among these men. Even though he wasn't like them, he seemed to enjoy their company.

Johnny still went back to Pennsylvania cider mills to get seeds in the following years. Once, he tied two canoes together and filled them with apple seeds and supplies and traveled home by river.

Many stories of this time involve Johnny surprising settlers by suddenly popping out of the woods. Sometimes he seemed to appear out of nowhere to say hello. At other times, he warned them of hostile Native Americans nearby.

The new United States government had decided that an area could become a state when its population reached sixty thousand. In 1803 Ohio became the seventeenth state. Johnny realized that central Ohio would become a major pathway for pioneers settling in the area and farther west. He began to focus on his Ohio orchards.

This ability to envision the future is what

made Johnny so important in the history of American settlement. He had a knack for figuring out where people were going to move to next. Before a big rush of people went to a new area, he somehow got there first and planted apple trees.

Other farmers gathered apple seeds from cider mills just as Johnny did. They planted orchards in the frontier, too. But most of them settled down next to their orchards. They built homes and began families. Johnny stayed on the move, planting as he went.

Over the years, he planted many orchards spread over three states. No one else did that.

The new Ohio state government began offering small areas of land for sale. When Johnny turned thirty-five, he had saved enough money to buy some. This was the first land he ever bought.

Johnny told his father about the rich farmland in Ohio. In 1805 his father moved the family to Ohio, settling near Marietta. Johnny didn't live with them. Marietta had been around for a while and already had enough orchards.

The Ohio Company wanted settlers to buy land in Ohio and stay there. So they made a rule.

Settlers had to plant fifty apple trees and twenty peach trees on every one hundred acres of land they brought. The company believed that settlers would be likely to stay once they had done so much work on a piece of land.

This rule was a lucky break for Johnny Appleseed. Ohio settlers were in a hurry to plant orchards. They were anxious to buy his seedlings.

Chapter 6
The Legend Blossoms

The first newspaper in the Northwest Territory was published in 1793 in Cincinnati, Ohio. But frontier settlers rarely got a chance to see a newspaper or any book besides the Bible.

Most cabins were built far apart, and settlers didn't get many visitors. So they were glad to see Johnny when he came to their cabins to advertise his apple business and sell apple seedlings. Besides, he didn't just bring seedlings. He brought news and stories.

Johnny was a good storyteller and liked to

entertain settlers with his wilderness adventures. He told of a life full of exciting escapes from bears, wolves, and other wild animals. He told of tending his own wounds with a piece of blazing-hot iron. And he told of the time he set his canoe on a large piece of ice floating down a creek. The ice carried him along faster than he could have paddled. Unfortunately, he fell asleep and wound up passing the place he'd meant to land.

When Johnny told stories, his gray eyes

sparkled. He knew how to use his voice to build a story to a thrilling climax or to make people laugh.

One thing that surprised people about Johnny was that he was always barefoot. He walked hundreds of miles in his apple business. His feet must have hurt at first. But the bottoms of them got tough after a while. Stepping on rocks and twigs became less painful. He occasionally stuck pins through the tough skin of his feet to impress people.

Some people wondered if his feet were magic. Rumors got started. It was said he could leap across rivers or melt ice with his bare feet. The soles of his

feet were said to be so tough that a snake's fangs couldn't pierce them.

People talked about his clothes, too. Some said he wore an upside-down cooking pot on his head! He made a brim for the edge of it to shield his eyes from the sun. He may have done that a few times. It would have been a good way to carry his cooking pot and to shade his face from the sun. But most of the time, he probably carried his pot in a backpack.

Johnny made his shirts out of empty coffee sacks with holes cut for his head and arms. Although he took baths, he didn't really care how he looked. He wore whatever he could find. Once, he found an old boot and a moccasin, so he put one on each foot.

Some Native Americans believed Johnny was a medicine man because he looked and acted so odd. They admired him and didn't try to hurt him.

Johnny met so many people through his travels that he became more and more well-known. Everyone who saw him remembered him. People who had never met him claimed they had, and made up stories about him. Pioneer families who knew him told his adventure stories to others. Some of the stories got exaggerated as they were passed around. The legend of Johnny Appleseed grew, as tall tales about him spread.

A tall tale is a story with exaggeration, adventure, and humor. Real-life problems get solved easily in funny, amazing ways.

Each group of workers in the old west had a tall-tale hero that made what they did look easy. Paul Bunyan was a logger. He helped settlers clear forestland for farms and cabins. Paul Bunyan was so strong he could pull trees from the ground with his bare hands, even when he was a baby!

As a boy, Paul Bunyan rescued a blue ox

from a snowstorm. He named it Babe, and Babe became his lifelong best buddy.

Pecos Bill was a Texas cowboy. According to the legend, his parents moved west when he was just a baby. As their covered wagon crossed the Pecos River, Bill fell out. He was rescued and raised by a family of wild coyotes.

With such a strange upbringing, Pecos Bill grew up to be a very unusual cowboy. When a rattlesnake bothered him one day, he used it to lasso a bull and invented cattle roping! Digging fence postholes was tiring. So he got prairie dogs to do it for him. He even tamed a wild horse named Lightning for an outlaw gang.

In time, pioneers began telling tales about Johnny Appleseed. In the days before television, telling stories about a folk hero was a favorite pasttime. But Pecos Bill and Paul Bunyan were not real people. Johnny Appleseed was.

Chapter 7
A Good Apple

A "good apple" is a nickname for someone who is a good person. Johnny Appleseed was a good apple.

Sometimes he helped settlers build cabins or chop trees. He knew they were struggling to make new lives for themselves in the west. If

people couldn't pay, he traded apple seedlings or gave them away for free.

Johnny usually brought gifts when he visited settlers' cabins. He loved children and brought them bits of ribbon or interesting things he found in the woods. Most pioneer children had only a few homemade toys. For fun, they rolled barrel hoops,

played with rag dolls, and rode ponies carved from wood. They were glad to get anything new to play with. Johnny also gave settlers herbs such as dandelion or catnip, which were used as medicine.

Polite settlers invited him to stay overnight in their cabins. Even when they offered him a bed, he insisted on sleeping on the cabin floor or outside on the ground. Sleeping outdoors was one of Johnny's favorite things to do. He covered himself with a blanket of leaves to keep warm. If the weather was bad, he would quickly build a crude hut or sleep in a hollow tree.

During his visits, Johnny read aloud from books he always carried. They were written by a man named Emanuel Swedenborg. The New Church was created to follow his beliefs. Swedenborg believed that helping others was a good way to find happiness. He believed in the importance of thinking for yourself and deciding how to live a useful life. Swedenborg believed people should not be afraid to be different. You can see why Johnny liked these ideas.

It's uncertain when Johnny first became interested in the New Church, but he was so excited about its ideas that he wanted to share them. Since he didn't own many of Swedenborg's books, he divided those he had into sections. He would lend one section to a pioneer family. Then on his next visit, he would exchange it for the next section of the book.

Johnny was a vegetarian, so he didn't eat meat served at settlers' dinner tables. He believed it was wrong to kill animals. Pioneers hunted for food and thought his belief was strange. While traveling in the forest, Johnny boiled creek water in his cooking pot, adding berries, grain, or potatoes to make a meal. He also may have taken some "journey bread" on his trips in the forest. This was bread that Native Americans taught him to make from corn.

There are many stories about Johnny's kindness toward wildlife. He fed squirrels and birds and released animals from traps. He bought abused animals and found people who would care for them. When he took honey from a beehive, he always left enough for the bees.

While pulling heavy wagons westward, some horses became lame. Settlers turned them loose in the woods. It was hard for the horses to find enough food and water. Each fall, Johnny would gather as many of these horses as he could. He would find someone to care for them through the winter. In the spring, he would lead them to land where there was better grazing.

Some people said he knew how to communicate with robins and turkeys. They said even wild deer would come when he called.

One popular story told of a snowy night when he decided to seek shelter in a hollow log. When he spied a mother bear and her cubs in the log, he didn't bother them. Instead, he slept out in the snow so they could keep warm in the log.

Johnny didn't even kill snakes or bugs if he could help it. Once, while clearing brush in a new orchard, a rattlesnake bit him. Without thinking, he quickly killed it. He felt terrible about it and didn't kill snakes after that.

While helping to build a road, he was stung by a wasp. The other workmen thought he was silly because he wouldn't kill the wasp. But Johnny said it hadn't intended to hurt him.

Chapter 8
Trouble

In the early 1800s, shiploads of new immigrants arrived on America's East Coast every week. They came from Germany, Ireland, Scandinavia, and other areas. Thousands of them moved west, taking over Native American hunting grounds. The pioneers chopped down trees and

SHAWNEE

built cabins and farms in their place. Settlers hunted and trapped animals the tribes needed for food. Native Americans had lived in the area for centuries. Now suddenly pioneers said the land belonged to them.

DELAWARE

Many of the settlers were Johnny's friends. But many Native Americans were, too. Johnny had learned a lot about life in the woods from them. In turn, they had shown him what to eat, what dangers to avoid, and how to survive in storms.

Fighting was common between settlers and Native Americans. It made Johnny sad that there was trouble between his friends.

It also worried him that more trouble had begun brewing between England and the United States. English ships controlled the seas, and they were seizing American ships. England also forced hundreds of American sailors to join its navy.

At first, the American government fought back by refusing to buy English products or sell American products to England. Then on June 18, 1812, the United States declared war on England—again!

The English army knew Native Americans were angry at the settlers. They asked the tribes to help them fight the United States. Some tribes agreed. This caused even more trouble between the Native Americans and the settlers.

During the War of 1812, forests were extra dangerous. Both Native Americans and English soldiers were now fighting the settlers.

One September night, settlers in Mansfield, Ohio, heard news that they would soon be attacked. Johnny volunteered to ride thirty miles

to Mount Vernon for help. He rode all night, warning other settlers along the way. Later, people remembered hearing him ride in the darkness, shouting, "Run for your lives!" One man was so scared, he did exactly that. But he forgot to put his pants on first!

Johnny didn't like fighting. If a settler wanted to fight, Johnny challenged him to a tree-chopping contest instead. At the end, the settler was too tired to be mad anymore. It was also a way to clear more land.

If Native Americans wanted to fight with him, he tried to hide. Once he escaped a group of Native Americans by lying down in a shallow creek for hours!

THE CONSTITUTION

THE WAR ENDED IN 1815. BY THEN, MOST OF THE TRIBES HAD BEEN FORCED FROM THEIR LAND IN OHIO. ALL THE FIGHTING MADE JOHNNY WANT PEACE EVEN MORE.

DURING THE WAR OF 1812, THE AMERICAN SHIP *CONSTITUTION* SANK A BRITISH WARSHIP. REPORTS THAT AN ENGLISH CANNONBALL BOUNCED OFF THE *CONSTITUTION* LED PEOPLE TO NICKNAME THE SHIP "OLD IRONSIDES."

TECUMSEH
(1768–1813)

TECUMSEH WAS A SHAWNEE CHIEF WHO TRIED TO UNITE ALL THE NATIVE AMERICAN TRIBES. TOGETHER, HE BELIEVED, THEY COULD STOP PIONEERS FROM TAKING THEIR LAND.

THE NEW AMERICAN GOVERNMENT MADE MANY PROMISES TO THE NATIVE AMERICANS. OFTEN, THE PROMISES WEREN'T KEPT. LAND WAS TAKEN FROM THE TRIBES THROUGH TREATIES. NATIVE AMERICANS RECEIVED LITTLE PAYMENT.

TECUMSEH TRAVELED THOUSANDS OF MILES, WALKING, CANOEING, AND HORSEBACK RIDING. HE TALKED TO MANY CHIEFS ABOUT JOINING HIM TO FIGHT THE SETTLER INVASION.

WHILE HE WAS GONE, AMERICAN SOLDIERS WENT TO HIS VILLAGE. HIS TRIBE DECIDED TO BEAT THEM TO THE ATTACK. THE BATTLE OF TIPPECANOE BEGAN AND MANY ON BOTH SIDES DIED. AFTER THAT, OTHER TRIBES LOST FAITH IN TECUMSEH'S IDEAS AND REFUSED TO BAND TOGETHER.

IN THE WAR OF 1812, TECUMSEH SIDED WITH ENGLAND TO FIGHT THE AMERICANS. HE WAS KILLED IN BATTLE IN 1813.

Chapter 9
Hard Work

After the war ended, Johnny began buying more land. Some of his orchards were less than an acre in size. Others covered hundreds of acres. He took care of his orchards all by himself for most of his life.

Sometimes he needed help for certain jobs. When he was forty-five, he hired two boys for a few days. They helped him build a one-room cabin on some of his wilderness land. Each night,

they shared his simple dinner, then slept on the ground beside Johnny's campfire. Wolves howled and owls screeched all around them. At first, the boys were scared, but Johnny told them not to worry. He was used to such things and knew the animals wouldn't hurt them.

Johnny's brother-in-law often helped in his orchards. However, none of Johnny's family knew how much land he owned or how much money he had. He sometimes buried his money among the roots of a favorite tree. He didn't trust banks.

America's banks got in trouble in the 1820s. Many businesses failed. Times were hard for Johnny, too. Squatters took over some of his land. And he also had trouble repaying some loans. He soon lost all of his orchards in Pennsylvania and many of those in Ohio. But he didn't give up.

Around 1830, he planted his first orchard in Indiana. By now most people knew him as Johnny Appleseed rather than John Chapman. In the following years, he bought 140 acres for only $250. He worked in his Indiana orchards for the rest of his life.

Johnny never got married or had children. Growing up in a noisy house as a boy may be one reason he preferred to live alone!

Still, there were many rumors about his love life. One says that he fell in love with a woman named Dorothy Durand. The story goes that she loved him, too. But their families kept them apart because they believed in different religions. Dorothy died of a broken heart. Johnny never got over her. He often returned to place apple blossoms on her grave.

In the last years of his life, Johnny owned

thousands of apple trees and lots of land, perhaps as many as twelve hundred acres. This didn't mean he was rich, but it's likely he was too busy to go go farther west. Besides, settlement on the West Coast hadn't gathered much steam yet. But who knows—if he had lived long enough he might have beaten settlers to the Pacific coast and planted apple trees there, too.

Johnny Appleseed did what he loved all his life. He grew apples, took long hikes, and never settled down in a home or owned many things.

As the years passed, he continued to roam, sometimes renting places to sleep in farmhouses. He was always traveling and probably spent ten thousand or more nights sleeping under the stars.

After walking through a snowstorm to care for some apple trees, Johnny got sick with pneumonia. He died in Fort Wayne, Indiana, on March 18, 1845, when he was seventy years old.

By the time Johnny died, there were twenty-seven states. He had planted orchards in three of them—Pennsylvania, Ohio and Indiana. They are shaded in gray on the map.

THE UNITED STATES 1844

The United States was a very different country from the one Johnny knew as a boy. In 1845 Texas became a state. The big migration along the Oregon Trail began right around the time that Johnny Appleseed died. The Gold Rush in California began in 1849. At that time, California still belonged to Mexico. But it became a state in 1850. Now the country went all the way from "sea to shining sea."

OHIO

PENN.

DISCOVERING NEW APPLES

ABOUT SEVENTY-FIVE HUNDRED KINDS OF APPLES ARE GROWN WORLDWIDE. APPLES CAN BE RED, YELLOW, GREEN, OR SOMEWHERE IN BETWEEN. SOME TASTE SWEET. SOME ARE SOUR OR TART. THE LIST OF MOST POPULAR APPLES INCLUDES McINTOSH, ROME, GRANNY SMITH, RED DELICIOUS, GOLDEN DELICIOUS, AND JONATHAN. THIS IS HOW SOME OF THEM WERE NAMED:

McINTOSH

IN 1811, JOHN McINTOSH DISCOVERED A NEW KIND OF APPLE ON HIS FARM IN ONTARIO, CANADA. HE NAMED IT THE McINTOSH RED.

THE ROME APPLE WAS DISCOVERED IN OHIO'S ROME TOWNSHIP IN 1816.

ROME

LEGEND HAS IT THAT MARIE ANN SMITH DISCOVERED THE GRANNY SMITH APPLE IN AUSTRALIA. IN THE 1860S, SHE THREW AWAY A PILE OF CRAB APPLES. A NEW KIND OF TREE SPROUTED FROM THE SEEDS. ITS GREEN APPLES WERE CALLED GRANNY SMITHS IN HER HONOR.

IN 1872, JESSE HIATT DISCOVERED AN UNUSUAL SEEDLING IN HIS APPLE ORCHARD IN PERU, IOWA. HE CUT IT DOWN TWICE, BUT IT KEPT GROWING BACK. IT FINALLY GREW INTO A TREE THAT PRODUCED PRIZE-WINNING APPLES. A JUDGE IN AN APPLE-TASTING CONTEST IN MISSOURI SAID THE APPLES WERE "DELICIOUS." THE LABEL STUCK, AND THE APPLES WERE CALLED RED DELICIOUS.

THE FUJI APPLE IS A POPULAR APPLE THAT WAS INTRODUCED IN 1962. JAPANESE RESEARCHERS BLENDED TWO KINDS OF APPLES TOGETHER TO MAKE IT.

FUJI

NEW KINDS OF APPLES ARE BEING GROWN ALL THE TIME.

Chapter 10
The Legend Lives On

Twenty-six years after Johnny died, an author wrote an article about him in *Harper's New Monthly Magazine*. It was called "Johnny Appleseed—A Pioneer Hero." Readers all over America enjoyed reading about Johnny's unusual life. Imagine a barefoot man roaming through the forest to plant apple seeds! Interest in him grew, and people wanted to know more about him.

Johnny didn't leave any letters or diaries behind to tell us about his life. Luckily, a few people were so interested in him that they did some detective work.

In the 1930s, a Leominster, Massachusetts, librarian named Florence Wheeler decided to find out more about his family. She studied records that showed who owned land in the area and the dates they bought and sold it. Through birth and death records, she found more information.

We now know the names of five generations of Johnny's ancestors. It turns out that he wasn't the first person in his family to love apples. His

great-great-great-grandparents grew apple trees in Massachusetts in the 1670s. And one of his relatives was a wealthy English count who did science experiments!

A woman in Ohio was interested in Johnny, too. Florence Murdock collected anything she found that was related to him. Her collection included articles that were published about him

and old letters that mentioned him. She even managed to preserve leaves saved from trees he actually planted! Today her collection is part of

the Johnny Appleseed Museum in Urbana, Ohio.

The legend of Johnny Appleseed continues to grow. Books and songs have been written about him. There are websites about him. In Leominster,

there is a school named for Johnny Appleseed. There is even an official Johnny Appleseed Trail in northern Massachusetts.

Every September, Johnny Appleseed festivals

are held in various towns. There are parades, games for children, and contests to see who can bake the best apple pies.

In Fort Wayne, Indiana, the Johnny Appleseed Memorial Park was named in his honor. A monument there marks what some people believe to be his grave. However, it's uncertain if this is really where Johnny was buried.

Most of the trees Johnny Appleseed planted are now dead. But seedlings from some of his trees are now growing outside the Johnny Appleseed Museum.

Many other trees grown from seeds produced by his original trees still exist in the Midwest. So the next apple you eat could be related to one of Johnny Appleseed's original apples!

APPLE FACTS

* AN APPLE TREE CAN GROW UP TO FORTY FEET TALL AND LIVE ONE HUNDRED YEARS.

* ABOUT 25 PERCENT OF AN APPLE IS AIR. THAT'S WHY APPLES FLOAT IN WATER.

* MANY APPLE FARMERS GROW DWARF APPLE TREES BECAUSE THE TREES USE LESS SPACE THAN LARGER ONES AND THE APPLES GROW CLOSER TO THE GROUND.

* A MEDIUM APPLE HAS ABOUT EIGHTY CALORIES.

* A BUSHEL OF APPLES WEIGHS ABOUT FORTY-TWO POUNDS AND CONTAINS ABOUT 115 MEDIUM-SIZE APPLES.

* THE BIGGEST APPLE ON RECORD WAS GROWN ON A FARM IN ENGLAND. IT WEIGHED 3 POUNDS 11 OUNCES AND WAS 21 1/4 INCHES AROUND.

* SIXTEEN-YEAR-OLD KATHY WAFLER MADISON MADE THE WORLD'S LONGEST UNBROKEN APPLE PEEL IN 1976, IN NEW YORK. IT WAS 172 FEET 4 INCHES LONG.

* APPLES ARE A MEMBER OF THE ROSE FAMILY.

* THE SCIENCE OF FRUIT GROWING IS CALLED POMOLOGY.

* AMERICAN COLONISTS SOMETIMES CALLED APPLES "WINTER BANANAS."

* APPLES ARE GROWN IN ALL FIFTY STATES. THE STATES THAT GROW THE MOST APPLES ARE WASHINGTON, NEW YORK, MICHIGAN, CALIFORNIA, PENNSYLVANIA, AND VIRGINIA.

* THE COUNTRIES THAT GROW THE MOST APPLES ARE CHINA, UNITED STATES, TURKEY, POLAND, AND ITALY.

* WHEN AN APPLE IS CUT IN HALF CROSSWAYS, YOU'LL SEE A FIVE-POINTED-STAR PATTERN AT ITS CORE. EACH OF THE FIVE SECTIONS HOLDS EITHER ONE OR TWO SEEDS. SO THERE ARE BETWEEN FIVE AND TEN SEEDS IN AN APPLE.

BIBLIOGRAPHY

Haley, W. D. "Johnny Appleseed, A Pioneer Hero." **Harper's New Monthly Magazine,** 43 (November 1871): 830–836

Hodges, Margaret. **The True Tale of Johnny Appleseed.** New York, Holiday House: 1997.

Kellogg, Steven. **Johnny Appleseed.** New York, William Morrow and Company, Inc.:1988.

Lawlor, Laurie. **The Real Johnny Appleseed.** Morton Grove, IL, Albert Whitman & Co.:1995.

Moses, Will. **Johnny Appleseed: The Story of A Legend.** New York, Penguin Putnam Books for Young Readers: 2001.

Price, Robert. **Johnny Appleseed: Man and Myth.** Urbana, OH: Urbana University Press: 2001. (originally published in 1954)

Warrick, Karen Clemens. **John Chapman: The Legendary Johnny Appleseed.** Berkeley, Enslow Publishers, Inc.: NJ, 2001.

To learn more about Johnny Appleseed or about apples, visit these sites:

The Johnny Appleseed Society and
Museum Bailey Hall
Urbana University
579 College Way
Urbana, OH 43078
www.urbana.edu/appleseed.htm

The Johnny Appleseed Heritage Center and
Outdoor Historical Drama
www.jahci.org

The U.S. Apple Association
www.usapple.org

Ohio Apples
www.ohioapples.org

New York Apple Association
www.nyapplecountry.com

Washington State Apple Commission
www.bestapples.com

TIMELINE OF JOHNNY APPLESEED'S LIFE

1774	John Chapman, later known as Johnny Appleseed, is born September 26, in Leominster, Massachusetts
1776	Johnny's mother and baby brother die
1780	Johnny's father remarries and moves the family to Longmeadow, Massachusetts
1797	Johnny moves west
1798	Johnny plants his first apple orchard in Warren, Pennsylvania
1801	Johnny plants his first apple orchard in Ohio
1805	Johnny's father and the rest of his family settle near Marietta, Ohio
1807	Johnny's father dies
1809	Johnny makes his first land purchase, in Mount Vernon, Ohio
1813	Johnny warns Ohio settlers of a suspected attack by Native Americans
1816	Johnny makes an Independence Day speech in Huron County, Ohio
1817	Johnny's missionary work is mentioned in a Swedenborg Church report in England
1828	Johnny describes himself as "a gatherer and planter of apple seeds" in a land deed
1830	Johnny plants his first orchard in Indiana
1845	Johnny dies on March 18 in Fort Wayne, Indiana, at the age of seventy
1871	An article about Johnny's life appears in *Harper's New Monthly Magazine,* making him famous around the world

TIMELINE OF THE WORLD

The Declaration of Independence is signed — **1776**

England signs the Treaty of Paris, ending the Revolutionary War — **1783**

The United States Constitution is approved — **1787**

The Northwest Territory is created and opened to settlement — **1787**

The Ohio Company establishes Marietta, Ohio — **1788**

George Washington is elected the first United States president — **1789**

Edward Jenner develops a vaccine to prevent smallpox — **1796**

French soldiers in Egypt discover the Rosetta stone, a key for translating hieroglyphics — **1799**

Beethoven finishes his first symphony — **1800**

Ohio becomes a state, the first in the Northwest Territory — **1803**

President Thomas Jefferson makes the Louisiana Purchase — **1803**

Lewis and Clark head westward on their exploration trip across America — **1804**

The War of 1812 begins between the United States and England — **1812**

French emperor Napoléon Bonaparte is defeated — **1815**

Author Mary Shelley writes the book *Frankenstein* — **1818**

The United States adopts a flag with thirteen stripes and one star per state — **1818**

Naturalist Charles Darwin reaches the Galápagos Islands on a ship called the HMS *Beagle* — **1835**

Davy Crockett and others die at the Alamo in San Antonio, Texas — **1836**

Charles Dickens's book *A Christmas Carol* is published — **1843**